The Lion
First Book
of
Bible Stories

To Nick, Daniel, and Alexander   B.V.

Text by Lois Rock
Illustrations copyright © 2011 Barbara Vagnozzi
This edition copyright © 2011 Lion Hudson

The moral rights of the author and illustrator
have been asserted

A Lion Children's Book
an imprint of
Lion Hudson plc
Wilkinson House, Jordan Hill Road,
Oxford OX2 8DR, England
www.lionhudson.com
ISBN 978 0 7459 6207 8

First edition 2011
1 3 5 7 9 10 8 6 4 2 0

A catalogue record for this book is available
from the British Library

Typeset in 17/20 Baskerville MT
Printed in China June 2011 (manufacturer LH17)

Distributed by:
UK: Marston Book Services Ltd, PO Box 269, Abingdon, Oxon OX14 4YN
USA: Trafalgar Square Publishing, 814 N Franklin Street, Chicago, IL 60610
USA Christian Market: Kregel Publications, PO Box 2607, Grand Rapids, MI 49501

THE LION
First Book
of Bible Stories

Lois Rock

ILLUSTRATED BY
Barbara Vagnozzi

LION
CHILDREN'S

Contents

In the Beginning   6
Genesis 1–2

The Garden of Eden   10
Genesis 2–3

The Great Flood   14
Genesis 6–9

Abraham and the Promise   20
Genesis 12, 15, 17, 21

Jacob and Esau   24
Genesis 24–25, 27, 29–33

Joseph and His Dreams   30
Genesis 37, 39–45

Moses and the People of Israel   36
Exodus 1–12, 14

Joshua and the Land of Canaan   44
Exodus 20, 24–25; Deuteronomy 31; Joshua 1, 3, 6, 13–19, 24

David and Goliath   50
1 Samuel 8–9, 17; 2 Samuel 2, 6

Jonah and the Great Fish   56
Jonah

Daniel and the Lions   62
Daniel 1, 6

Jesus and the Kingdom of God   66
Matthew 1–2, 4–5, 7, 10; Mark 1, 3; Luke 1–2, 4, 6; John 1

A Storm at Sea   72
Matthew 8; Mark 4; Luke 8

The Wheat and the Weeds   74
Matthew 13

The Hole in the Roof   76
Mark 2; Luke 5

The Good Samaritan   80
Luke 10

The Runaway Son   84
Luke 15

An End and a Beginning   88
Matthew 21, 26–28; Mark 11, 14–16; Luke 19, 22–24; John 11–12, 18–20

In the Beginning

In the beginning, there was… nothing.

Now, you can think of wide, wild oceans, imagine dark and stormy seas.

But back then, there was nothing: wide, wild nothing; dark, stormy nothing.

And God.

Into the nothing, God spoke:

"Let there be light."

And there was: light like the good news to come, full of hope and promise. God called the light "day" and the darkness "night". And that was the very first day.

Then God spoke again.

"In the middle of all that is nothing, let there be space for something."

The space uncurled and swirled and spread.

It grew high and wide like the blue-domed sky.
And that was the second day.

On the third day, God told the land to rise up from the sea.
"From the earth," whispered God, "let the green plants grow."
The seedlings unfurled and trees grew tall.

There were bright flowers, ripe fruits, and fields of nodding grasses.
On the fourth day, God spoke to the heavens:
"I want the golden sun to shine through the day.
"May the moon be its mirror through the silver-lit night.
"Let bright stars glitter around."

On the fifth day, God spoke again.

"In the sky, let there be birds.

"Birds that soar, birds that shriek, and birds that sing.

"In the seas, let there be mysteries: flitting fish, mighty whales, and weird and wonderful tentacled things that ripple in the tide."

Then came the sixth day:

"Let there be beasts, bold and bellowing.

"Let there be creatures shyly hiding.

"Let there be insects, buzzing and humming, and all manner of things that make their homes in nooks and crannies and crevices.

"And finally," said God,
"I shall make people.
"They will be in charge of
the world and take care of it.
"There will be something
of me in each of them.
"And they will be my friends."

On the seventh day, God
and all the world rested.
Everything was made…
and it was wonderful.

The Garden of Eden

God made the first man and called him Adam.

God planted a beautiful garden in Eden to be Adam's home. The garden was a paradise: full of beautiful trees that bore fruit just perfect for picking.

"Everything is for you to enjoy," God told Adam. "You can live here and be happy.

"There's just one thing to remember. Look over there – that tree in the centre. Its fruit is harmful. Don't even think of eating it. It will kill you."

So Adam lived peaceably in the garden. The animals were his friends, and God made the first woman to be his wife and companion.

Her name was Eve.

One day, as Eve was walking alone through the garden, she heard a rustling.

She looked around and… what was that, half-hidden in the shadows? It was a snake, quite bold, and it was gazing at her, unblinking.

"Thisss tree, thisss tree here."

Eve was astonished. The snake was talking to her.

"Did God say not to eat its fruit? Surely not. It's the best."

Eve tossed her curls. "Don't put silly ideas into my head," she said. "If we eat that fruit, we will die."

"Nonsense!" said the snake. "It's sensational – it will make you wise. How odd that God wants to keep secrets from you."

"Oh," said Eve. She thought for a moment. She reached up. She picked the fruit and bit into it.

"Mmm!" she said. "Come over here, Adam. You simply must try this fruit."

Adam bit into the fruit and closed his eyes. "That's wonderful," he said.

Then he opened his eyes. "Oh, it's making me feel odd. Scared, kind of."

"You're right," said Eve. She hugged her arms tight around her. "I feel… exposed."

They joined hands and sheltered under a tree whose leafy boughs reached low.

There, through the afternoon, they wove its leaves into garments. They were hoping to protect themselves from… from some new and unnamed danger.

But the tree could not hide them, nor the leaves protect them. That evening, God came and found them, and God knew.

"The fruit has done its worst," sighed God. "Danger, dying, decay. I had hoped you would never know about these things, but it is too late. You don't belong in this garden now. The world beyond must be your home.

There, you will
have to work for all
you need – from this day
to the day you die."
God dressed the man and
woman in animal skins and sent
them out of the garden. An angel
stood at the gate, wielding a sword.
The blade flashed so brightly that Adam
and Eve could not even see paradise.
"We must make of our lives what we can,"
they agreed. But they were deeply sad.

Would they ever
be friends with
God again?

The Great Flood

Years had passed since the first man and the first woman had stepped into the world. There had been children and grandchildren and their children and their grandchildren… on and on.

The world was full of people. It was also full of trouble. Bickering. Arguing. Sneering. Bullying. Fighting. It was quite dreadful.

God was very unhappy. "I'm sorry I made people," said God. "There's only one good man alive: Noah. I shall go and talk to him.

"I'm going to send a flood," explained God to Noah. "It will end this bad old world. But I need you to build a survival boat: an ark. It will be for you and your family…

"Oh… and a male and a female of every kind of animal.

"It's a big boat. Let me give the measurements."

Noah started work.

He and his three sons built the boat.

Noah's wife and his sons' wives gathered the food.

Together, they gathered the animals, and the animals all marched in pairs.

"It's time to shut the door," said God. "Here comes the rain."

It rained and rained and rained and rained
until there was nothing left of the world.
There was just a flood – and an ark.
It floated through the rain.
It floated through the drizzle.
It kept on floating as the clouds blew away.
And then one day…
BUMP.

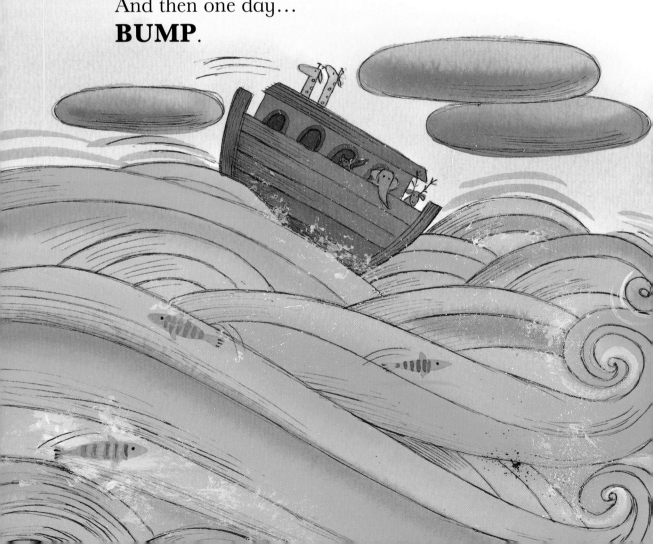

"We're on a mountain top," said Noah. "We might as well wait here until other mountain tops appear."

As the flood began to go down, Noah opened a window and sent a raven to look for land. It flew away and didn't come back.

"Unhelpful bird," muttered Noah. "Let's see if the dove can do better."

The first time the dove flew out, it soon came back. Then, seven days later, Noah sent it out again. It came back with a fresh olive leaf in its beak.

"Wonderful news," said Noah. "The plants are growing again somewhere. We won't have long to wait now."

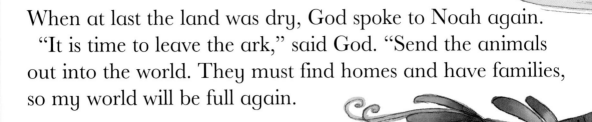

When at last the land was dry, God spoke to Noah again.

"It is time to leave the ark," said God. "Send the animals out into the world. They must find homes and have families, so my world will be full again.

"And I will bless your family. You will have grandchildren and great-grandchildren, and their children will have children for ever.

"Look at the sky. The rainbow is a sign of my promise. Never again will I send a flood like this one. For as long as the world exists, there will be summer and winter, seedtime and harvest."

Abraham and the Promise

Long ago lived a man named Abram. He could trace his family all the way back to Noah, but there was a problem.

He had no children of his own. "Perhaps my family ends with me," he sighed. "Neither I nor my wife Sarah is getting any younger."

One day, God spoke to Abram.

"Tell your wife and your nephew to get ready. Command your servants and your slaves to get busy. Have them round up your flocks and herd your cattle. It is time to go on a journey. I am going to lead you to land that you can make your home.

"And this is my promise: there you will have children. Your family will become a nation. They will be my special people. They will help everyone in the world to understand that I am God. The whole world will see the good things that I will do for them."

So Abram started out. He left the city with its tall buildings and paved streets.

He became a tent-dweller in the land of Canaan. When he found pasture for his animals, he set up camp. When he had stayed in one place as long as he could, he and his household moved on.

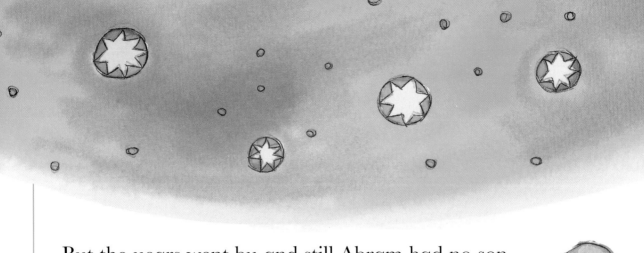

But the years went by and still Abram had no son.
His nephew had children.
His slaves had children.
One night, as Abram was sitting glumly under the starlit sky, God spoke again.

"Believe in my promise. You will have a son. Your family will be as many as the stars in the sky.
"Now I am going to give you a new name: Abraham. It means you will be the father of many nations."

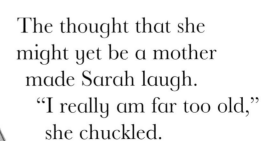

The thought that she might yet be a mother made Sarah laugh.
"I really am far too old," she chuckled.

But God's promise was true. At long last, she and Abraham did have a child.
He was overjoyed.
She was overjoyed.
They named the little boy Isaac, and the name means "laughter"

Jacob and Esau

Abraham's son Isaac grew up, and the time came to find him a wife. A servant was sent to ask Abraham's relatives, far away, if they could suggest the right girl. Together they chose a beautiful young woman named Rebecca. When Isaac saw her, he fell in love with her, and they were happy together.

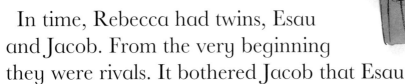

In time, Rebecca had twins, Esau and Jacob. From the very beginning they were rivals. It bothered Jacob that Esau had been born first: even though he was only slightly older, he was going to be the one to inherit the family wealth.

Isaac was proud of Esau. The young man was strong and a good hunter. That meant plenty of meat for the stews Isaac loved to eat. Rebecca doted on Jacob. He stayed at home and helped with the cooking.

One day, Esau came back from hunting feeling hungry.

"I'd love some of that soup," he said to Jacob.

"Only on one condition," replied Jacob. "A bowl of soup for your rights as the older son."

Esau was too hungry to argue and he agreed.

Later, when Isaac was old and about to die, he sent Esau hunting for something to make a last, delicious stew. "Then I will say a prayer, asking God to bless you when you are head of the family," he said.

Rebecca overheard. While Esau was out, she and Jacob made a selfish plan. They made goat stew instead, and Jacob went to his father pretending to be Esau. Isaac said the blessing prayer. Jacob had tricked Esau out of everything.

When Esau found out, he was very angry.

"I'll kill that sly, cheating so-called brother of mine!" he raged.

Rebecca knew he meant it, and she was scared.

"Hurry," she warned Jacob. "Go and stay with my brother, your uncle Laban, far away."

So Jacob went.

Uncle Laban knew that relatives must take care of each other. He agreed that Jacob could work for him, looking after his flocks of sheep.

He agreed that Jacob could marry his lovely daughter, Rachel – as long as he put in seven years' unpaid work first.

Jacob did the work. But at the wedding, Laban dressed Rachel's older sister as the bride and tricked Jacob into marrying her first.

Now Jacob was **furious**.

"Local custom, my boy," said Uncle Laban. "You can marry Rachel as your second wife next week.

"As long as you put in another seven years' work after."

And so it went on. Laban kept trying to cheat Jacob out of any pay. Jacob hit on a clever plan to accept as pay any black lambs and speckled or spotted goats born in the flocks. Then he made sure he bred as many of that kind as possible and made himself wealthy. The two men quarrelled bitterly. In the end, they had to agree to part.

Jacob had nowhere to go but his old home.

That was a bit of a problem. Going home would put Jacob within reach of Esau… and meeting him might prove unpleasant. "That is what I deserve," he thought ruefully, "given how I cheated him."

He made a plan. "I have plenty to give as gifts to Esau," he told his servants. "Cattle, donkeys, sheep, goats, hard-working slaves. I want you to go to tell him and ask if these will please him…

"Please him enough not to want revenge on me."

The servants started out, but all too soon they were back. "Your brother… he'd found out already. He's on his way here with 400 fighting men."

Jacob was very scared. He tried to think of ways to keep his family safe, but he knew that there was no escape for him.

He was going to have to go and meet Esau.

Jacob bowed low as he saw his brother. He knew it was only right for him to ask forgiveness. But Esau simply came running up to sweep his brother into a big hug.

"Good to see you, you old rascal," he laughed. "How are you? What can I do to help you get going again?

"My goodness… and here's your family. Pleased to meet you, everyone!"

It turned out that God had blessed both the brothers, and there was room for both of them to live in peace.

Joseph and His Dreams

When Jacob's family was complete, he had twelve sons.
Two of these were the sons of his favourite wife, Rachel.
The younger was Benjamin. The elder was Joseph.

And Joseph was Jacob's pride and joy. He arranged to have
a splendid coat made for him, richly decorated.

"So now it's obvious," sneered the ten older brothers.
"Our father is going to give Joseph all the best of everything.
As if he were the eldest son."

Joseph didn't make things better. "I had a dream," he told
his brothers. "We were harvesting sheaves. My sheaf stood up,
and yours bowed down to it."

"Oh really," replied the brothers. "You can be sure
WE won't be doing any bowing."

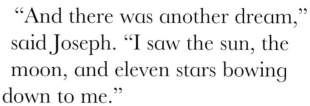

"And there was another dream," said Joseph. "I saw the sun, the moon, and eleven stars bowing down to me."

That made even Jacob angry.

"If you think that your eleven brothers, your mother, and your father are going to bow down to you, you'd better think again," he said.

But Joseph's boasting had made his brothers furious.

Not long after, Jacob sent the ten older sons to go and look after his flocks. When they had been away some time, he asked Joseph to go and check they were all right.

The brothers saw Joseph in his amazing coat and their anger exploded. They ripped off Joseph's coat and made a plan to get rid of him. By the end of the day, they had sold their brother to slave traders.

They dirtied the torn coat. Then they went to tell Jacob that Joseph had been eaten by animals.

In faraway Egypt, no one thought that Joseph was special.

He was just a slave. He found out what it was like to work hard. Really hard.

He found out what it was like to be treated unfairly. His master's wife told lies about him and he was thrown into prison.

He found out what it was like to sit in prison, feeling forgotten.

But God had not forgotten Joseph. He gave him the wisdom to explain dreams.

When the king of Egypt had a puzzling dream, someone sent for Joseph.

"Listen to what I dreamed of," said the king. "None of my so-called wise men know what it means."

But Joseph did.

"You say you saw seven fat cows, and then seven thin cows that ate them.

"You say you saw seven fat ears of grain, and then seven thin ones that ate them.

"The two dreams mean one thing: there are going to be seven years of plenty, and seven years of famine.

"You should choose someone to store the extra grain from the good years to last through the bad ones."

The king eyed Joseph thoughtfully.
"That's very good advice," he said.
"I choose you to do the job."

After seven years, the stores of grain
were full. When famine struck,
Joseph was in charge of selling it.
One day, ten brothers came
from far away, desperate to buy.
Joseph knew who they were –
but they did not recognize him.
Joseph spoke angrily,
demanding to know all
about them. He was
anxious to hear about his
father… and his own full brother, little Benjamin.

"Now you must prove your story," he snapped. "One of you
must stay here in prison. The rest must go and get Benjamin."

When Jacob heard this demand, he was dismayed. "I can't
lose Benjamin," he wept. "Not after what happened to
Joseph."

But there was no choice. The family needed food.
Benjamin was taken to Joseph, and Joseph made a plan.

He had a silver cup hidden in Benjamin's pack of grain.
He sent the brothers on their way, and then sent his
servants to go and accuse them of stealing.

They were all dragged back to Joseph.

"Benjamin is the thief. He will be my
slave," he declared.

Another brother stepped forward.
"Keep me instead," he said.
"Our father Jacob will die if
Benjamin has to stay."

Then Joseph knew: they were
sorry. And he could hold back
no longer.

"Look at me," he cried. "I'm Joseph! God took care of me so
I can take care of you now. Go and fetch our father. Come
and live in Egypt."

And so the broken family was mended.

Moses and the People of Israel

In Egypt, the sons of Jacob became
a nation: the people of Israel.
There came a new king of
Egypt, who was wary of them.
"We Egyptians need to keep
control here," he told his officials.
"Make those foreigners our slaves."
But still the people of Israel grew in number.
"Seize their baby boys," ordered the king.
"Throw them in the river."

One mother was not going to let that happen.
She made a basket and covered it with
waterproof tar. She cradled her baby inside

and went to hide it in the tall reeds by the river's edge.

"Keep watch," she whispered to her daughter, Miriam.

As Miriam watched, she heard chattering. A princess of Egypt was coming with her servant girls to bathe.

The princess saw the basket. A servant took it from the water so she could look inside.

"Oh, it's a baby!" she said. "I want to keep him safe. I shall name him Moses. Now all I need is someone to look after him for me."

Miriam stepped forward. "I can find someone," she said. She returned with her mother. The princess was delighted and asked her to look after Moses.

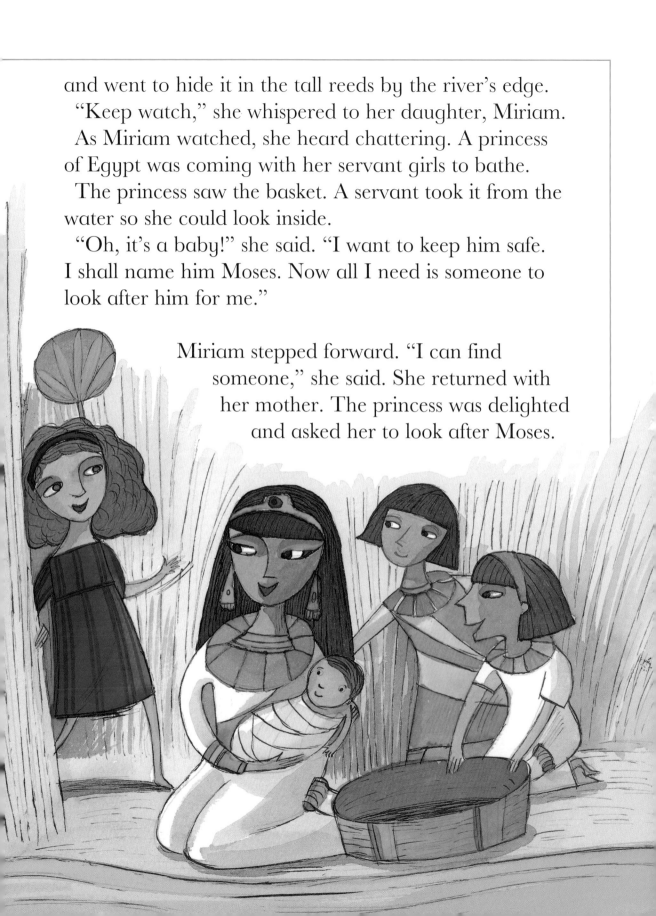

Moses grew up as a prince of Egypt. But he knew he was also one of the people of Israel.

When he was a young man, he went to see how they were faring. He was shocked to see how hard they had to work. He was so angry he got into a fight with a slave-driver and killed him. Then he ran away.

In the wild country, Moses became a shepherd. One day when he was out with his flocks, he saw a bush flickering with orange flames. But there was a mystery: the bush was still alive… it wasn't being burned up.

Then he heard a voice: "I am God: the God of Abraham," it said. "You stand on holy ground.

"Moses: I have chosen you to go back to Egypt. Tell the king to let my people go free."

Moses protested. "I won't be any good at that," he said. "I always stumble over my words. The king won't pay me any attention."

"Go and find your brother Aaron," said God. "He will do the talking. And I will make you perform miracles that will show the king my power."

So Moses and Aaron went and spoke to the king of Egypt.
"The God of the people of Israel says this: let the people go."
The king's answer was clear: "No."
Moses and Aaron did not give up. "It is God who wants the people of Israel to be allowed to go," they told the king.

"If you do not agree, then all kinds of disasters will strike."
And so it was. First the river turned blood-red and the fish all died.
Then came the frogs: frogs that hopped everywhere. Frogs that died and began to stink. "The people of Israel stay," growled the king.
Then came clouds of gnats and swarms of flies. A mysterious disease made all the animals die. Another gave the people awful boils that would not heal.

A hail storm flattened the crops and broke branches off trees.

After that, a plague of locusts came flying in from the desert. People heard the rattling sound as they swarmed in and ate every bit of green leaf.

Then the sky turned dark and stayed that way for three days.

Moses gave the king a final warning. "God will change your mind. The next disaster will be the worst. In a single night, all the firstborn will die."

Moses gave instructions to the people of Israel. "Get ready to leave Egypt. On the night I tell you, prepare a special meal with quickly made bread that doesn't need to be left to rise. Roast a whole lamb, and mark your doors with its blood.

"Death will strike the firstborn in the unmarked houses of the Egyptians. You will be safe: death will pass over."

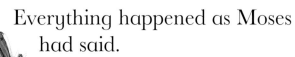

Everything happened as Moses had said.

The night of death put the king into a frenzy. "Go! The whole lot of you," he told Moses. "Take what you like but get out of Egypt."

Moses and the people of Israel hurried away, feeling both scared and excited at what lay ahead for them.

They had been gone for some time when the king suddenly changed his mind. "What have I done!" he exclaimed. "I can't afford to be without those slaves."

He frowned at his army officers: "Get the chariots ready AT ONCE," he ordered. "We're going after them."

The people of Israel were camped by the Red Sea when they saw the army: the chariots glinted gold amid the cloud of dust thrown up by galloping horses.

"Don't be afraid," said Moses. "Watch to see what God will do."

He held his staff high. At once a strong wind began to blow. It blew a path through the sea: dry land where there had been water. The people of Israel hurried through.

Behind them the Egyptian army came thundering.

But when the people of Israel were safe on the other side, the wind stopped and the water flowed back.

The Egyptian army was swept away. Moses had led the people of Israel to freedom.

Joshua and the Land of Canaan

When the people of Israel escaped from Egypt, their leader was Moses.

One day he went alone to the top of a mountain named Sinai. There, he listened as God gave him ten great laws – commandments. There were laws about loving God. There were laws about how people should love one another.

"Remember to keep these laws," Moses said. "They are your side of an agreement with God: a covenant. God will be your God. You will be God's people, and God will bless you."

The great laws were written on tablets of stone. The people made a golden box in which to keep them safe: the ark of the covenant.

But years went by before the people were ready to claim Canaan as their home. By then, Moses was old and he knew he didn't have long to live.

He gathered the people together. "Today I am choosing a new leader," he said. "I am choosing someone who is strong and brave. I am choosing someone who is willing to obey all of God's laws.

"I am choosing Joshua."

Joshua was soon making plans to enter Canaan. First the people must cross the River Jordan.

Joshua told the priests to lead the way, carrying the ark of the covenant. As they stepped into the Jordan, the waters dwindled to a trickle. All the people marched across.

45

Next the people of Israel had to claim the land.
   The first task was to capture the fortress city of Jericho.
   "God has given me a plan," said Joshua.
"Let's make a procession.

"First, an advance guard of soldiers.

"Then seven priests with trumpets.

"Then more priests carrying the ark of the covenant – for God's laws must be at the heart of all we do.

"Finally, more fighters to bring up the rear."

Once a day, for six days, the procession marched around the walls of Jericho.

On the seventh day, the procession marched around **seven** times.

Then the priests blew the trumpets. The people gave
a **shout**.
The walls of Jericho fell down, and the people
of Israel captured the city.

It was the first of many victories. When the land was won, Joshua decided who should live where. Each of the great families of Israel was given a place to call home.

When Joshua was old, he gathered the people together.

"Here we are, safe in the land our God promised us in the time of Abraham.

"Through the years, God has taken care of us. We must live as God's people.

"As for me and my family, we promise to obey God's laws. What will you do?"

And all the people replied: "We will obey God's laws."

David and Goliath

When the people of Israel first settled the land of Canaan, they believed God was looking after them.

But it wasn't always easy to make a living from farming; bad weather could ruin the crops, and harvests could simply fail. In the bad years, the people began to worry. Perhaps their God wasn't all-powerful. Perhaps they should say prayers to the gods of the land of Canaan too. Surely it couldn't do any harm?

But it could: to do so was to disobey God.

As they no longer had God's blessing, the enemy people all around came raiding and plundering their land.

In time, the people wanted a king who would lead them in battle. The choice fell on Saul.

So it was that Saul found himself leading an army against the Philistines. They even had strong iron weapons and gleaming bronze armour.

More than that, they had a champion soldier: a giant of a man named Goliath.

"Who dares fight me?" Goliath roared at Saul and his army. "Beat me, and you win the war."

It so happened that a young shepherd boy was there. His name was David, and he had come from his home in Bethlehem to visit his soldier brothers.

"I dare," he said.

"You're only a boy," said King Saul. "What could you do against Goliath?"

David shrugged. "I can protect my sheep from wild animals. If God can keep me safe from bears and lions, God can help me beat that boastful Philistine."

"At least take my armour," said Saul.

David tried the armour, but he couldn't even walk in it. "I'll fight the way I'm used to," he said.

So David took off the armour. He picked up his stick. He chose five smooth pebbles from the nearby stream and put them in his bag. He got his slingshot ready and went to meet Goliath.

Goliath laughed: a giant laugh.

"Do you think I'm a dog, coming at me with a stick like that?

"Ha ha ha ha haah!"

"You've got a sword and a spear and a javelin," said David. "But I come in the name of God."
He fitted a pebble into his slingshot.
He whirled it around and…

Threw.

The pebble hit Goliath so hard that he toppled over.
David raced up and grabbed Goliath's own sword.
"I win," cried David.

The Philistines left Goliath to his defeat,
and ran away.

David became a hero.

Years later, after Saul had died in battle, David became king.

He chose Jerusalem to be his great city. He had the ark of the covenant brought there in a great procession. He made plans for a beautiful temple to be built on the hilltop there.

And he wrote songs of praise to the God who had kept him safe all through his life.

Jonah and the Great Fish

King David brought his people peace and prosperity.

It was not to last. As before, the people of Israel forgot to obey God's laws.

Away to the north was a mighty empire, ruled from its capital city. Its rulers planned to conquer the world. Everyone trembled at the mention of the people of Nineveh.

But now listen to the story of Jonah. He was a prophet, and God came and spoke to him, saying: "I know that the people of Nineveh are wicked. I want you to go and warn them."

Jonah got up at once. But he didn't go to Nineveh. Instead, he hurried down to the port of Joppa. He paid his fare to travel on a boat bound for Spain. He went below deck and fell fast asleep.

When the ship was far out at sea, God sent a violent storm. The sailors were terrified the boat would sink. "Everyone on deck!" they cried. "All hands to work!"

But the storm grew worse. "This is punishment from some great god," they whispered. "Who on board is to blame?"

They drew lots to find out: it was Jonah.

"I confess," said Jonah. "I'm running away from God. Just throw me into the sea."

The sailors were dismayed, but they had no choice.

Jonah began to sink: down, down, down.

Gulp.

From somewhere in the murky depths, a great fish came and swallowed Jonah.

From deep inside the creature's belly, Jonah said a prayer. It was a long prayer, but it really meant one thing: "Help."

The fish swam close to shore and belched Jonah onto the beach.

"I think you know how to get to Nineveh from here, don't you?" said God. "Remember the message I wanted you to take."

Jonah hurried to the great city at the heart of the evil empire.

"Change your ways," he cried. "Turn away from wickedness… or the great God of heaven and earth will destroy you for ever!"

"Oh dear!" said the people.

"Oh dear!" said the king. "Suddenly it all seems so clear.

"Listen, everyone: we must mend our ways. We must tell God we are sorry. Then perhaps God will forgive us."

And God did.

Jonah was very angry.

"I knew you'd do that," he said to God. "That's why I wanted to go to Spain. If I hadn't warned the people of Nineveh, you would have had to punish them. It's exactly what they deserve."

Jonah left the city and built himself a little shelter, waiting to see what would happen to Nineveh. God made a plant grow: it twined itself around the roof and shaded Jonah with its leaves. "Lovely," said Jonah.

The next day, God sent a worm. It chewed the plant so it died. The sun rose, bright and hot, and Jonah felt wretched.

"This is awful," he moaned. "My poor plant!"

God came and spoke to him.

"Jonah, why are you so doleful? What right do you have to feel sorry for a plant? You didn't plant it. You didn't make it grow."

Jonah picked up a wilted leaf and tried to fan himself.

"Try to understand," said God. "You know what it is to feel sorry for something. Well, I felt sorry for Nineveh: its people, its children, and all the animals."

Daniel and the Lions

The people of Israel were only a small nation. Around them, emperors went to war to make themselves rulers of the world.

On one occasion, the ruler of Babylon marched to Jerusalem and destroyed it. Captives were taken to Babylon. Among them was a man called Daniel.

Daniel was honest and wise. He became an adviser to the king. Even when a new king, Darius, came to the throne, Daniel was given an important job.

There were other advisers who grew jealous. They watched

to find a fault in Daniel. Then they went to King Darius.

"O King, may you live for ever. May all your subjects give respect to you alone.

"Test their loyalty: make a law forbidding anyone to ask the favour of anyone else – human or god.

"Say that anyone who disobeys will be thrown to the lions."

Darius was flattered. He made the law.

The advisers went to spy on Daniel. "There he is again," they chuckled. "Praying to his God."

Then they returned to the king.

"O King-may-you-live-for-ever: ghastly news.

"Daniel has broken your law. It is a terrible thing to say but you have no choice.

"THROW HIM TO THE LIONS."

King Darius knew he had been trapped. Sorrowfully, he gave the order. To Daniel he simply whispered, "Only your God can help you now."

Darius spent a sleepless night, fretting for Daniel.

But God did help Daniel.

An angel came and sat in the pit with Daniel and the lions, and the lions did Daniel no harm.

When Darius found out that Daniel was still alive, he was overjoyed.

"Go and bring Daniel back from the pit," he ordered his soldiers. "Then go and get the real villains.

"And now, I am going to send a new message throughout my empire. I will tell everyone that the God of Daniel is the living God, the one who will rule for ever."

Jesus and the Kingdom of God

The people of Israel, now known as the Jews, always believed that God would bless them and, through them, all the world.

After many wars, they were able to rebuild their country: their homes, the city of Jerusalem, its beautiful Temple.

Above all, they believed that, one day, God would send a king like David. He would rule with peace and justice. His kingdom would never end.

The announcement, when it came, was a quiet one. God sent an angel to a little town called Nazareth. The angel had a message for a girl named Mary.

"God has chosen you to be the mother of his Son," said the angel. "He is God's promised king. You will name him Jesus."

At that time, the land of the Jews was ruled by an emperor in Rome. He gave the order that everyone in his empire had to go to their home town. There they were to put their names on his list of taxpayers.

So it was that Mary went with Joseph, her husband-to-be, to the town of Bethlehem. There, Jesus was born.

Angels told shepherds that God's king had been born. Wise men followed a star to bring him royal gifts.

Jesus grew up in Nazareth. From Joseph he learned to be a carpenter. Nobody in the town thought he was special.

But Jesus knew that God was his true Father, and one day he began the work for which he had been born.

He went from Nazareth to the rest of the region of Galilee. He began preaching to anyone who would listen.

"The time has come," he told them. "The kingdom of God is near. Listen, and I will tell you more.

"To be God's people, you must do more than obey the law. You must love as God loves – even your enemies.

You must forgive as God forgives – even those who do you wrong."

Many came to listen. Rich people and poor people; some who were popular and others who had no friends; some who were strong and others who were ill or disabled; grown-ups and children.

Some he chose to be his special friends: disciples.

"So what does it mean," said Jesus, "if you listen to my words and obey them?

"You will be like the wise man, who built his house on rock.

"The rains came, the rivers flooded, while around the storm winds blew.

"But his house stood firm. It was quite safe, because it was built on solid foundations.

"And what does it mean," said Jesus, "if you listen to my words but do not obey them?

"You will be like the foolish man, who built his house on sand.

"The rains came, the rivers flooded, while around the storm winds blew.

"His house began leaking. His house began creaking.

"Then **CRASH!**

"His house fell down. And what a terrible fall that was!"

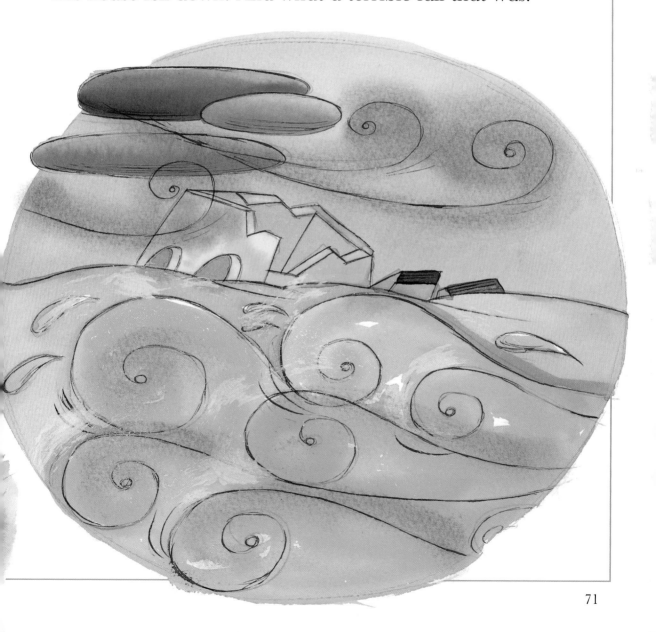

A Storm at Sea

Jesus lived in the region of Galilee, and nestling among the hills was a large lake: Lake Galilee. Jesus had chosen four disciples from among the men who fished in its waters.

One evening, Jesus asked his disciples to sail him across to the other side of the lake. He was tired from his day of preaching and soon fell asleep, his head on a pillow.

When they were a fair way from land, a sudden storm blew up. The boat began to rock violently, dipping and plunging like a wild monster. Waves crashed over the sides, drenching the men and puddling at their feet.

"Everyone help!" cried one of the fishermen. "We could go over any minute.

"And wake Jesus up. Doesn't he care?"

Someone shook Jesus from his sleep. He sat up and gazed at the scene of chaos. Then he stood up. He called out to the waves: "Be quiet." He whispered to the wind: "Be still."

At once, the sea was calm. Jesus turned to his friends.

"Why were you scared?" he asked. "Have you no faith?"

The men went about their work, silent and shaken. "Who is this Jesus?" they asked. "Even the wind and waves obey him."

The Wheat and the Weeds

"Listen to this story," said Jesus. "It will help you understand what the kingdom of God is like.

"There was once a man who sowed a field. He chose good seed: it promised a fine harvest of wheat.

"Soon the seeds began to grow, their slender green shoots reaching for the light.

"But the man's servants saw something else, and they went to tell their master.

"'We know that the seed you sowed was the finest; but there is bad news. All kinds of weeds are growing among the wheat. Do you want us to go and pull them up?'

"'Leave them,' replied the man.

74

'If you pull up the weeds, you might damage
some of the wheat.

"'Let them grow together until harvest time.
Then I will tell the workers to pull out the weeds,
gather them in bundles and burn them.

"'After that, they will gather the wheat and put
it safely in my barn.'"

The Hole in the Roof

Through all the region of Galilee, people were talking of Jesus.

The news about him was astonishing.

"He can work miracles," they said. "Sometimes he just touches a person, and they are healed. Sometimes he just says the word, and people come back from death's door."

"I won't believe it until I see it!" said some.

"I wouldn't want to see it," warned others. "What power can he be calling on to do that kind of thing? I find it quite… disturbing."

One way or another, there were lots of people who wanted to see Jesus.

And when people heard that he was in a particular house, crowds came to see if they could get near enough to see him.

Of course, there were sick people who wanted to see Jesus too. They had a very real reason for wanting to know if he could work miracles. And on that day, four men had made a special effort to take their friend to him. The friend could not walk, so they carried him, using a blanket as a stretcher.

But the crowd was already spilling out of the door of the house, and no one would let them through.

"Time for problem-solving," said one.
"When one path is blocked, it's time to find another.
The outside steps take us onto the roof. It's easy to break
through the ceiling – and a simple job to repair afterwards."
  So the friends made a hole in the roof right above the place

where Jesus was. Then they let the man down on his blanket.

Jesus could see at once how much faith the men had in him. He spoke to the one who could not walk:

"Your sins are forgiven," he said.

Around him, the faces of several of his listeners wrinkled into frowns. "Only God can forgive sins," they muttered. "Who does Jesus think he is? This kind of talk isn't proper."

Jesus smiled at them. "Which is easier to say?" he asked. "'Your sins are forgiven' or 'Get up and walk'? I will prove that I am able to do both."

He spoke to the man again. "Get up, roll up that blanket, and walk home."

To everyone's amazement, he did just that.

The Good Samaritan

There was once a man who went to Jesus with a question. "One that will test him!" he chuckled. "One that will find out if Jesus deserves to be called a teacher."

And so he asked: "What must I do to win eternal life?"

Jesus saw the ruse. "You've studied the great books of our people," he replied. "What do they say?"

"Ah, the great commandments," declared the man – who was himself a teacher. "They can be summed up in two: love God with all your being; love your neighbour as you love yourself."

"Quite right," said Jesus. "You knew the answer already."

The man was taken aback. He had been found out and felt quite foolish.

"But who is my neighbour?" he blustered.

Jesus told a story.

"A man was going from Jerusalem to Jericho. Miles of empty road wound through the hills. There, in a bleak and lonely place, robbers came and attacked him. They beat him, robbed him, and left him for dead.

"It so happened a priest of the Temple in Jerusalem was going that same way.

"'A dead body,' he whispered to himself. 'How... deeply unpleasant.' And he hurried by on the other side.

"Then a Levite, an official of the Temple in Jerusalem, came by. He walked up to the man for a closer look. Then he shook his head and hurried by.

"Then came a third traveller: a man from Samaria. And as you know, those foreigners have nothing to do with the Temple in Jerusalem – so what can they know about worshipping God?

"The Samaritan saw the man. He walked over to him. He bandaged his wounds. He lifted him onto his donkey and took him to an inn.

"There, he took care of him.

"The next day, he had to travel on. So he took two coins and gave them to the innkeeper.

"'I am paying you to look after my injured friend,' he said. 'If it costs more, I will give you the extra next time I am here.'"

The story over, Jesus smiled at his questioner.

"So," he said, "who was the neighbour to the robbers' victim?"

The man frowned slightly. The story made him feel… well, uncomfortable.

"The one who was kind to him," he snapped.

"Then you go and do the same," said Jesus.

The Runaway Son

Among Jesus' friends were the friendless: the not-like-us people; the do-they-do-that people – the wrong kind of people.

Among Jesus' enemies were quite decent people. Honest, law-abiding, definitely religious… and more than a little bit smug.

"How can Jesus help people know about God?" they grumbled. "Look at the company he keeps!"

Jesus told a story.

"Once there was a man who had two sons.

"The elder was dutiful and hard-working and loyal. He put in long hours on the farm alongside the servants.

"The younger dreamed of riches. 'I want to go and have fun now,' he whined to his father. 'Why do I have to wait until you're dead to get my share of the family fortune?'

"The father was sad, but he felt he had no choice. He divided his property between his two sons. The younger went and sold his share, took the money, and went travelling.

"In a country far away, he lived his dream: idling in the day, partying at night.

"Soon his money was gone. Then came crisis. The harvests were poor and the price of food shot up. The young man tried to find a job – anything to make a living.

"A local farmer took pity on him. He hired the young man to look after his pigs.

"It was depressing work, sitting in the dust, with smells and flies all around. And he still couldn't afford enough to eat: he was tempted to eat the pig food. Then he came to his senses.

"'My father treats his servants better than this. I shall go back to him and say how sorry I am. I'll ask to be his hired worker.'

"So he trudged the long and weary miles. He was still a long way off when he heard a shout – and the sound of running. 'My son! You're back! How happy I am to see you.'

"It was his father, hugging him tight.

"'I'm sorry,' the young man said. 'What I did was wrong: utterly wrong. I don't deserve to be your son.'

"But his father wasn't listening. He was calling for the servants. 'Quick – fresh clothes, proper shoes – dress this man like the guest of honour. And let's have a party – no expense spared.'

"The elder brother was out in the fields. He heard music and dancing. He asked a servant what the party was for. He did not like the answer.

" 'My good-for-nothing brother! After all he's done! While I worked and worked – and you never even offered to let me have my friends round for a good roast dinner.'

"The father was dismayed. He came to plead with his son. 'Everything I have belongs to you. But your brother was lost, and today is found.

" 'It is right to be glad and to celebrate.' "

An End and a Beginning

It was a fine day in spring. Jesus and his disciples were going to Jerusalem for the festival called Passover. Many other people were making the same pilgrimage.

Jesus asked his disciples to bring him a donkey so he could ride the last few miles. As he did so, the crowds began to notice.

"It's Jesus. The miracle worker. The one who preaches about God's kingdom."

"Perhaps he's going to declare himself king in Jerusalem?"

Someone gave a cheer. Then the whole crowd started shouting. "Here comes the king! Hallelujah!"

Some spread their cloaks to make a carpet on the path. Others waved palm branches as if they were flags.

Jesus entered the city and went to the Temple. The courtyard was bustling. In fact, it was a marketplace for the festival – traders shouting their wares, buyers haggling over prices.

Jesus watched, his expression both angry and sad. Suddenly he overturned one of the tables. Then another… and another.

"Out, the lot of you," he cried. "This place is meant to be a house of prayer. You have made it a den of thieves."

The priests and the Temple officials were furious. But there was nothing they could do. For Jesus began coming to the Temple to preach, and the crowds were eager to listen.

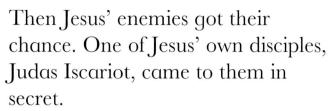

Then Jesus' enemies got their chance. One of Jesus' own disciples, Judas Iscariot, came to them in secret.

"I could tell you where to find Jesus alone," he whispered. Then leaning closer he added, "If your price is right."

The deal was done: a life for thirty pieces of silver. And Judas acted as if everything was normal as he and the other disciples made plans for the festival meal.

He sat with them all at the table. Together they recalled the story of the festival: the covenant made in the time of Moses – the promise that God would be their God, and they would be God's people. Then Jesus took some bread and shared it with them.

"This is my body, broken for you," he said.

He took the cup of wine and passed it around. "This is my blood, poured out for you," he said. "It is the sign of God's new covenant.

"Remember always to share a meal like this, and remember me.

"Know this for sure: the time for my body to be broken and my blood to be spilled is near. Someone here will betray me."

Not long after, Jesus and his friends went to a quiet olive grove to sleep. Judas slipped away, bringing armed men back with him. They arrested Jesus and took him to his enemies. The disciples simply ran away.

Jesus was put on trial. The priests accused him of treating God without respect. Then they dragged him to the Roman governor, Pontius Pilate. They told him that Jesus was a rebel who planned to set himself up as king.

Pilate did not really believe them, but outside his palace a mob had gathered. They were demanding that Jesus be put to death.

That day, on a hill outside the city wall, Jesus was crucified. Just before sunset, a small group of friends came and took the body. Hurriedly they laid it in a tomb.

Night fell. The next day was the sabbath, when work was forbidden. Then came another dark night.

Early in the morning, some women went back to the tomb. They wanted to say a last goodbye. But something had happened. The stone door that had been rolled in place to seal the tomb was open. The body had gone. Suddenly, two angels stood before them.

"Don't look in a tomb for someone who is alive," they said. "Jesus is not here. God has raised him to life."

The women went back to the disciples, full of wonder. They told their tale, but no one believed them.

But later that day, while they were in a room together, Jesus appeared.

"Peace be with you," he said.

"As God sent me to this world, so I now send you.

"Let God strengthen you with the Holy Spirit.

"Tell the world my message. Tell people to love and forgive one another, and God will love and forgive them.

"Then they will be part of God's kingdom: God's friends for ever."